Until The End Of Time

Edited by

Heather Killingray

First published in Great Britain in 2002 by
POETRY NOW
Remus House,
Coltsfoot Drive,
Peterborough, PE2 9JX
Telephone (01733) 898101
Fax (01733) 313524

Copyright Contributors 2002

HB ISBN 0 75432 770 1
SB ISBN 0 75432 771 X

FOREWORD

Although we are a nation of poets we are accused of not reading poetry, or buying poetry books. After many years of listening to the incessant gripes of poetry publishers, I can only assume that the books they publish, in general, are books that most people do not want to read.

Poetry should not be obscure, introverted, and as cryptic as a crossword puzzle: it is the poet's duty to reach out and embrace the world.

The world owes the poet nothing and we should not be expected to dig and delve into a rambling discourse searching for some inner meaning.

The reason we write poetry (and almost all of us do) is because we want to communicate: an ideal; an idea; or a specific feeling. Poetry is as essential in communication, as a letter; a radio; a telephone, and the main criterion for selecting the poems in this anthology is very simple: they communicate.

A deep Winters Love
on page 144.
Written by:-
    Susan Carole Roberts.

CONTENTS

I NEVER KNEW

As a little girl I used to dream.
I used to hope and used to think,
About what I would be
And what I would see.

I hoped that I would be happy,
That I would shine like a star,
But little did I know that
Men with guns would take lives.

I never knew that they would kill,
I never know that they would torture,
I never knew that they would be so heartless and cruel.
I just knew, I hoped my life would be happy!

But what a surprise did I get!
I saw the real world
The world of fear,
The world of murder!

Hermina Duratovic

At The End Of A Rainy Day

The headlights did their best
to pierce the gloom
Which ebbed and flowed
And choked the street
And the room
was all unmade - a jigsaw
Missing a Christmas tree
or a picture was mislaid
And life now moved
to a jerky
1920s beat
As the rain fell
softly on the street
- And pale blank faces will look up
emerge from a coffee cup
And listen to some anecdote
before reaching for a coat
And standing on a doorstep, fumble
for words to fit, finally mumble
Goodbye and turn and leave
A silence fit for any grave
But not an end
just a change
at the most
Say boy to man
Say girl to woman
Say Father and Son
and Holy Ghost
and admit defeat . . .
The wind crept
slowly down the street
and still the rain persisted

Resistance was hopeless
For you
The war is over
at last
How swift the years
How swift they pass . . .

John Thomson

RECAPTURE

Thank you.

I was passing
Through
Consciousness,
When you
Woke me up
To the world.

Oblivious
Of life.
You bounced
My bubble
And let it burst
Over experience.

Like Ariel,
I was freed
From that tree.
Free, liberated.
But still under
Power.

Your art
Hypnotised
My creative dreams.
Now I'm flying
Transfixed,
Around your island.

But I will never
Be free.
True liberty
Will never be mine.
Your art
Lies in my mind.

Bound to you
Like the mermaid
And the sea.
Never being able
To run.
Free.

But I'm going
To fly,
In your ocean.
Until
The pirates come.
Thank you.

Rebecca Culpan

SLEEP

I want to sleep
But about my bed
Ghosts and phantoms
Are wandering.
In the corner of the room
They're peering at me
From behind a bookcase
That's no longer there.

Now they're floating round
The ceiling, casting evil spells
Just to keep me awake.
I wonder what they'd do
If I just closed my eyes
And fell into the arms
Of Morpheus?

Vicky Stevens

EXISTENCE

Can you connect
a single particle
with Mount Everest
the Atlantic
an elephant
a man
a spider
a tiger
the Earth
a mother
Saturn
a bumble bee
the Moon
a magpie
the Sun
Venus
the Galaxy
a grasshopper
the Universe
a baby
Big Bang
and everything
in existence?

Everything and all things
are linked
as partners
of the evolving life
of the Cosmos . . .
the macrocosm
the microcosm.

Stephen Gyles

AUTUMN

As I sit here the summer was a blast,
But as autumn comes those days are past,
Those long hot days spent in the sun,
They become distant memories as autumn has begun.
Summer has many things to offer you and me.
The long evening and warm weather really suit to a tee.

Others like the sport, the hols and the sun,
Time spent with family there is so much fun.
Don't get me wrong I love autumn too,
But the days are shorter and the sky is not so blue.
The rain increases and the garden is a mire,
But this gives us a chance to light a good turf fire.

As smoke from the fire rises to the sky,
I think of Cassies' custard and warm apple pie.
The autumnal scene is really a wonder,
Trees stripped naked and leaves lie asunder.
As the season moves on towards Hallowe'en,
The autumn and winter become a team.

It's not just as cold as the days in December,
But it's not as warm as before that I remember.
The winter breaks off and goes it alone,
Autumn moves away to find a new home.
It's always needed somewhere else in the world you see,
Until next year my friend - if God spares me.

J Curmas

To Dream A Little While

The cat lays long
The radiator warm
Look at this cat
She has no worries
Of day and world
She is provided for
Her hair combed - her catty dinner digested
Given not because she is so pretty
She cleans her paws; washes behind her ears
She is content - to lie asleep
She has done her work
Perhaps she has chased the odd mouse
Grateful as we are not to have them in the house
When she ventures into the wild out of doors - what adventures
We neither see, nor do we know
If she comes - she deserves her rest
If now we see - she rests - lo - she has dreams
Why should she not
We should all be able
- To dream a little while.

C J Bayless

THE DISGRUNTLED GNOME

Under a toadstool a wee elf sat
Scratching his nose and wiggling his hat
He was very angry this tiny wee elf
For the fairy queen had summoned him to report to her by himself!
'Why do I have to do everything?' she said he mumbled
As from under the toadstool he slowly tumbled.
At last he stood before the fairy queen
She was very angry because she had seen
That this tiny elf was so selfish and lazy
Always grumbling about something, flicking the daisies
That grew in profusion on the lawn, lifting small faces to the sun
'Wee elf I am very disappointed in you' said the queen
'You mumble and groan and whinge through the day
Paying no heed to what I say, well from now on I will tell you
Pull your socks up stop grumbling and moaning
Do something nice for a change, help other elves worse off than you
Try being like them and do the things they do'

Wee elf lowly bowed before his queen
He was so ashamed he didn't want to be seen by the other elves
Who stood obediently by, they knew wee elf would try to be good
Slowly he turned and bending low retraced his steps
Through the long castle hall, his footsteps echoing long
Then suddenly, he broke into a merry song
He sung to the beautiful fairy his queen
Now all the other elves joined in the singing
The fairy queen looked on, then said to herself
'Well done, well done my naughty wee elf!'

Irene Hartley

FEELING LOW

I sit alone at night,
by the table lamp light,
I try to convince myself it's alright,
but I know,
this feeling won't go,
I don't want to feel so low.

What can I do,
What can I say,
What can I change,
To make this feeling go away?

By myself, alone at night,
I sit and cry,
by the table lamp light.

J Cross

LITTLE BOW

Little Bow can travel through aeons of our time,
with eyes that read the soul he looks
at things that make you pine,
because he is now one of the great Sons divine,
so, he can tell you that your life has rhyme.

When you just think a question he answers you so fine,
and when he talks of people from the past,
his fund of knowledge makes you stand aghast,
but, when he looks at you your thoughts combine.

Healing is for him a spiritual path,
cupping your hand in both of his you feel a power glow,
and as he looks at you you really know,
what it is like to live without the wrath.

This man was all the medicine,
his tribe would ever need,
the whole life-giving creed,
the greatest of his line.

Jean Paisley

ANDY MOTORCAR

M itsubishi, Mazda, Mini, Mercedes and MG

O mega, Opal and a car name Odyssey

T riumph and Toyota turning around

O rion, Escort, Fiesta you're homeward bound

R enault and the Rover found

C hrysler, Citroen are all past in

A lfa Romeo, Audi, Aston Martin and Austin

R over land and lair Andy Rolls Royce only Justin

P Brewer

MEMORY LANE

In the twilight of my years I sit beside the fire
And think back to the bygone days, my heart filled with desire.
The country walks, the village fair, the toffee apple stall
Bluebells sway in Borsden Wood; yes, I remember them all.
Our little village baker made penny loaves to sell
Cooked rice pies, fruit loaves, big meat pies, gingerbread as well
The hardware store was packed with goods, a real Aladdin's cave
Sold paraffin in pink and blue for lamps our dad had made.
Our soft boiled eggs had lions on - the coal fire burned so bright
Mum washed our clothes in dollytubs, 'cause money was so tight
But we had fun and we had love, not like it is today
Neighbours popped round for a chat to pass the time of day.
Late at night we'd gather round the hearth so nice and warm
Whilst Dad would work such long hours seeing to the farm
Mum would warm our school clothes on a maiden by the fire
And make us dolls with string and wool and pegs with bits of wire.
Some people call them 'Bad Old Days', the work was long and hard
Mopping steps with donkey stones, sweeping our back yard
Now I sit here wondering where my life has gone
And think of all the happy days, what I've achieved and done.
But as I look around me, and all the mod cons here
My memory slips back in time and I gently shed a tear
The kids have grown and flown the nest and now I live alone
My only link to sanity is talking on the phone.
With a life that's nearly over through tired eyes I see
A young girl laughing happily, yes, that young girl was me.

P Bradley

BROKEN GLASS

I loved the broken glass on the convent wall
Glittering like jewels in the Summer sun,
Blood red rubies, emeralds, diamonds embedded in concrete
to protect the nuns.
Religious teachers of my youth had cutting tongues,
Wore jet black skirts that swept along the floors,
Lived in a twilight world of ordered hours
And long, lavender scented corridors.
The nuns have gone, the place is due for demolition.
No need to scale the walls, the gates gape wide.
Even the chapel's stained glass has been stoned,
Vandals have torn down boards and sneaked inside.
Children who never suffered that regime pollute the building
like a foul disease.
At a shattered bedroom window a lace curtain
Like a tattered petticoat, floats on the breeze.
Above the great front door Saint Brigid's statue
Views Knocklayde mountain with an envious eye,
Overlooks the convent garden where Spring stirs
Because the goddess Brid is passing by,
Prancing barefoot to an ancient pagan tune.
Where her cloak brushes leafless boughs of blackthorn bloom.
Where her feet pass, wild rabbits nibble grass and flowering currant
burgeons in the gloom.
The autopsy begins as salvage men move in, at least the parasites
are put to rout.
With surgical precision the cadaver is dissected and everything of value
taken out.
On Knocklayde's slopes cloud shadows flit, they never will pin down
the nebulous soul.
The crystal bowl's fragmented, its pieces hurled apart.
For me some shards will always shine engulfed within the life blood
of my heart.

Clare McAfee

HAROLD THE HORSE

Harold the horse was a snob you see,
he would trot round the field saying 'just look at me,
my coat is so shiny, my teeth are so white,
and I stand above others, just look at my height.'

He thought he was clever, not a hair out of place,
if he ran with the others he would soon win the race,
he would say to the horses 'My you do look rough,
not like me who is healthy, I don't huff and puff.'

But very soon Harold was to have a fright,
it would happen to him in the dead of night,
as the rain lashed down and the storm set in,
the fear of this night was to frighten him.

As the lightning struck and the earth seemed to move,
the others took cover but Harold would prove
he was not frightened and trotted along,
till it went very dark and something was wrong.

He couldn't move, as he thought 'I am sinking,'
'Oh dear' said Harold 'this needs quick thinking.'
But his legs thrashed about, this way and that,
he was stuck in the mud near the river in fact.

As his strength was sapping, he thought, 'What a mess,
I'll shout for the others, I need them I guess.'
So he shouted for help as loud as he could,
but the river was rising and so was the mud.

'Where are they?' he wondered 'why haven't they come?'
'Oh dear' thought Harold, 'what have I done?'
'I need all my friends in the field right now,
Oh please come and help me I'll change somehow.'

Then just as he gave up, the horses appeared,
they had heard his cries and it's just what they feared.
They had made the farmer come to his aid,
as the farmer got ropes and Harold was saved.

From that day on Harold was never the same,
he felt very humble, and very ashamed,
but the others forgave him for being a pest
now he trots round the field just like the rest.

Brenda D Volanthen

NURSERY TALES

Mary had a little lamb its fleece was white as snow,
and everywhere that Mary went she can no longer go.
For it would seem a virus is sweeping o'er the land,
little lambs like Mary's must join the growing band.
Tom Tom the piper's son has stolen his last pig
It's lying in a trench, that the army's had to dig.
Along with lots of others pink and so inert,
bundled one on top of each blemished with the dirt.
Little boy blue can blow his horn hard as he can blow,
his herd is on a funeral pyre, uttered their last low.
The sheep are in the meadow lying in a heap,
haystacks' soaked in chemicals, he's got nowhere to sleep.

Ring a ring a roses, a rhyme from long ago
another plague swept across the land,
scything people low.
Maybe in the future we'll other rhymes intone,
telling how we lost our livestock, in the year 2001.

Cough a pig and sneeze a cow the smoke gets up your nose,
woolly sheep, the 'dance and song' has taken all of those.
A pocket full of tissues to waft the smoke away,
ministry's a mystery, will be till judgement day.

Soldier soldier in the grass, rifle at the ready,
aim bravely twixt lambkins' eyes, squeeze the trigger steady.

Derek B Hewertson

IT'S HER LIFE

'Well that was it, her mind made up
That was the way, she'd live from today

Living her life
In a way, her own way
Ignoring the trends, not doing what was right
I mean 'socially' right.

Ignore the past and start today,
Living the proper way
A way she wanted, a way she dreamed
Living her life, the free way

Forget where she'd come from
Live for now and her own freedom
Her life was hers, for her to live
Not long now, till the end

Getting close
Is what it seemed
A day passed growing long
She didn't have time for growing old

For this is it
A sudden end.'

Jodie Lees

WINTER

I love the bitter cold
on frosty mornings.
Hot food warms me up,
before facing into the sharp air,
wrapped up in handknit jumper,
scarves and long skirt
around my ankles.
The blood circulates down
to my toes,
as I walk along the canal bank
and into Merrion Square,
ready for a day of typing
and constant calls.

or

I slowly come to life
walking by the canal bank,
absorbing the sounds of water,
the tingling of reeds in the breeze.
The fresh air prepares me
for a tedious day ahead,
behind the desk, typing, filing,
keeping bosses happy,
and customers content.

Mary Guckian

DREAM

Dream of a sunlit sky,
Let time flow.
Wonder at a tearful dewdrop,
Let thoughts slip by.
Watch the silent opening and closing of a rosebud,
Let reality disappear.
Smell the lasting fragrance of memories,
Breathe in and hold it in.
Peer through crystal, clear waters,
Close your eyes.
Remember cascading thoughts,
Surround yourself with nothingness.
Live a fantasy, stop and feel paradise's warm breath.
Dream!

Sadie England

THE GREAT UNIVERSAL

The train speeds through the old lands
competes with the new roads.

Faster and faster through the county of Cheshire
leaves behind misshapen trees of crooked old men,
guardians no more.

The green fields blur by.
The old gods, forgotten forever.

The new gods hide.
The black tarmac snake emerges
Swallows all that lives.

Older than the soul is the fight
not to be consumed by the emptiness of it all.

Roman Suchyj

CAKES OF THE DEVIL

Bony fingers sieve bronzed flour
In a world of discontent.
Assorted bitter fruit, peeled
and shelled, await a hopeful crumble.

Eggs fresh from the university fold
Are violently whisked in a froth
Of religious ideology, who search
For a martyrdom of milk.

Essential salts of understanding
are omitted from devil rich mixture
and placed in a tin of turmoil
to cook slowly with devilish taste.

Alex Branthwaite

BEFORE THE PRISON HOUSE

Childhood is:

A Beginning -
   usually quite unremembered by the main participant,
Family -
   and its private, personal world,
Cuddling -
   by and of people, animals and soft toys indiscriminately,
Sublime Ignorance -
   of the trials and tribulations to come,
Wonder -
   without judgement, at the newly unfolding world,
Delight -
   in the detail which greater knowledge and familiarity will obscure,
Love -
   which can be taken for granted without offence,
Security -
   in that food, clothing, shelter - and money - are someone
                                                    else's problem,
Trust -
   before the disillusionment of deceit and betrayal take hold,
Fantasy -
   before cold reality banishes the fairies and Father Christmas,
Games -
   and the endless, enviable, renewable energy to play them,
Leisure -
   to roam, to dream, and to explore, untroubled by time,
Laughter -
   as full and free as the tears which inevitably follow,
Freedom -
   from responsibility, if not minor constraints,
Summer -
   which is the only season - at least in retrospect,
Friendship -
   of a special, enduring kind, won by the pain of partings,

Learning -
    before it turns from fun to fear of failure,
School -
    which is something of everything,
A time -
    which is too eagerly cast aside by unappreciative children,

All too fleeting.

J M Potter

ME AND MINE

If only I could call you up
Or reconstitute your ash remains
I'd tell you of the harm you've done
Not to your friends
But to me and mine

You always gave the third degree
You never set ambition free
You were bitter
And how we felt it
You were the ice
That never melted

Alan Wilson

RELEASE

Satire saddled surrealist slander
Vengeance vented venomous verse
Acrid atrocities alluring affinity
Divided devotion derailing democracy
Realism rhetoric role-play renaissance

Mollycoddled maimed myth mottled
Tenacity tainted tolerance trust
Poignant proposition prowess premonition
Wilting wilderness waning will
Collate coercion contempt class

Benevolent banter blatant brash
Fundamentally forlorn faith flaying
Opulence opinions orator oppressed
Nepotism nonchalant naive notoriety
Environment evaporating exclude elitist

Applaud assertion avoidance aversion
Gigantuant global gathering grief
Hypocrisy heralds hierarchy hope
Irrelevant insane insearch invein

Michael Berry

MY LITTLE FRIEND

When I switched the light on, there I saw
This tiny little spider, crawling up my wall
I found it rather strange, he wasn't there before
I watched him watching me, as he began to fall
Catching this wee creature, oh so very slight
For, so afraid was I, my fingers he might bite
Safely in glass prison, this little thing's marooned
Curled up like a ball, all fluffy and brown
Staring straight at me, through crystal painted bars
I release him in the garden, beneath the winter's stars.
Moving away his prison's door, soon I'd send
Him scurry towards the undergrowth, farewell my little friend.

Ann Hathaway

THE RIVER PATROL

With the swift as the wing commander,
And the swallows in the ranks below,
The sand and house martins,
Complete the flight of the river patrol.

Stream-lined and graceful,
With agility, they've been blessed,
Eaves-droppers, from birth,
In flight from leaving the nest.

Acrobats of the air,
Who defy the wind its speed,
Glide and dive across the waters,
In a fly-borne effort of feed.

Africa knows of their presence,
On long distance sorties, they can be found,
Until the clock of the year marks time,
And once again they're homeward bound.

Bakewell Burt

SPECIAL PEOPLE

John Grant an only child
lived a life fairly wild
His precious parents gave him the chance
to grow develop, even to dance

The road in life is never straight
it twists and turns lies in wait
Some of us can take a wrong turn
family and friends are the ones we spurn

For a gifted few we get back on the road
a long hard struggle, each carry a load
Of guilt and remorse, with help from friends
we must put it behind us lest it never ends

With help from family and people who care
I know for this man he had to share
Share his time help others in pain
with love in his heart and nothing to gain

There is many survived who took the wrong road
a result of John Grant to help where he could
So thank God above for the ones who are good
to see others through the way that they should . . .

Jean Tennent Mitchell

EX-MUSICA

Went there to view the autumn
but discovered the magic of spring
delighting in the sun
within the gardens
stinging the skin
hot rays
memorabilia
but pale companions
of her
whose dance
was holy
rhythm
stringed harp
with each
tuned
angelically
the other

Séamas M. Ó Dálaigh

THE GHOST

Do you believe in ghosts
I do, I saw one
It was the ghost of a dolphin
Ha, you may laugh
But it's true, I did

We were on holiday in Greece,
One dark eerie night I couldn't sleep
Then I saw this white shimmering dolphin
Float to the door then disappear

I don't mind you laughing
I believe what I saw
The truth really is stranger than fiction
Hang on, there is much more

Next day I walked in the ruins of Apollo
And Delphi's ancient amphitheatre
Then walked along looking down on the Aegean Sea
Then it happened, I froze,
I had funny sensations up and down my body

My body was being drained
I felt but did not see,
All my blood was flowing away from my feet
I then felt a surge of new life
New beginnings for me

Hetty Foster

GOING ON

As the tear falls from my eye,
As the summer turns to rain,
As the little robin redbreast returns to my home once again.
As you look towards the sky,
You can see the mountains standing high.

As the river flows forever,
As the night turns to day,
As we grow older our hair will turn to grey.

As the love that's in my heart will stay forever,
As one life is gone,
There will be a new one born.
As today is history buried with the night,
Step out into tomorrow with the morning light.

Sylvia Brown

FREE-WRITING

This is a nice thing to do.
Just write as the tide wishes.
Anything might come out:
from breadcrumbs to the state
of civilisation.
And it does.
Despite bad world trends,
we have to carry on regardless,
making toast and the like.

Keith Murdoch

ABANDONED

An abandoned dog, I came across.
Lying on a carpet of moss.
Tired and hungry, feeble and weak.
If only this poor dog could speak.
I stroked his head, he licked my hand.
He sat up straight, without command.
He placed his paw upon my shoe
With thoughts 'Can I come home with you?'
I helped him up to stand at my side.
'I'll lead the way, I'll be your guide.'
I took him home to tend his need.
With a loving home, and, a nourishing feed.
His big brown eyes were very sad
To abandon an animal makes me mad.
Dogs are for life, not just for a season.
They love and respect without a reason.
I tended to him night and day.
With warmth and love in every way.
I can't explain the way I feel.
He never survived his tragic ordeal.

Catherine Fleming

VOLCANO

Trapped in an ageless desire
Application carried with scorn
Modified words to try and conform
Everything depending on form
Hoping to grasp the nettle
With the usual stamp of approval
Not so much of late but why?
Death and blood on our streets
The laugh outside is a welcome face.

Mulachy Trainor

TOTAL STRANGERS

If out of work, the poster said,
Then join the armed forces,
Enjoy good health, and learn a trade,
We have extensive courses,
You're fed up living off the state?
Or longing for adventure,
Then join us now, it's not too late,
To plan a better future,
They make it sound like so much fun,
And never mention dangers,
Nor do they say, you'll have a gun,
For killing total strangers.

Matthew L Burns

AWAY TODAY!

I didn't have much schooling
Yet, caught up pretty quick
And despite my constant fooling
I turned out far from 'Thick'.
I won a prize for 'Progress'
And chose a book on Birds.
Was never great on maths and stuff
But had quite 'a way' with words.
With art I found my natural flair
Though, my teacher felt inclined
To say I'd never make it big
With such a 'Far too tidy mind;
Cookery? Well, not quite so bad,
Yet, my sponge cakes wouldn't rise!
Mrs Scrafton lost her patience
Saying 'Perhaps you should stick to pies!'
Now, I must admit, I hated school,
And so, was not its keenest fan.
Nor of our own 'Ted Baker',
The 'School Attendance' man!
I legged it through the strawberries!
On many a sunny School day,
And once he'd caught me 'at it'
There was nothing I could say!
Perhaps I should have attended class?
And gained lots of GCEs?
Could that have helped my worries pass?
And saved these 'Housemaid's knees!

Rosanna Wright

RULES, RULES, RULES

Rules, rules, rules!
Mum said to me you know the rule,
So why are you trying to play the fool?
My teacher said you know the rule!
You don't seriously think it makes you look cool!
My sister said you know Mum's rule!
You should not jump into the paddling pool!
Dad said to me you know my rules!
So why are you using my gardening tools!
Gran said to me you know my rule!
Stop tormenting the kitten with my good wool!
My brother said you know Dad's rule!
Don't you try to bunk off school!
Rules, rules, rules!

Charley Gavin (11)

MY GRANDAD

My Grandad said 'Give me that thumb!'

My Grandad let me help pick his potatoes;
we gave them to Grandma

My Grandad tickled me a lot
it made me giggle and it was fun!

My Grandad told me funny jokes

My Grandad loved me lots

I thought my Grandad would last forever

I was sad when Grandad died

I am still very sad

I cried when Grandad died

Charlotte Byrne (8)

THE GREAT BED OF WARE

When did they remove the Great Bed from Ware
For I visited Ware but it was not there,
And if it was not in Ware it must be somewhere.
During the day the folk of Ware sold their wares
And at night eight folk slept in the Great Bed of Ware,
All wearing long night shirts, the in thing to wear,
Slumbering through nights in the Great Bed of Ware.
Now over the years the Great Bed of Ware
Began to show signs of tear and tear,
Then nobody slept in the Great Bed of Wear.
For it was taken away but I do not know where
To where artisans repaired the Great Bed of Ware,
And today in the V and A is the Great Bed of Ware
Restored to its former state but beware,
For no one now sleeps in the Great Bed of Ware.
All you can do is just stand and stare at where
Eight people once slept in the Great Bed of Ware.

David A Garside

Let Go Of Tension And Woe

Time to retire, what a night, wind whistles, howls with a powerful gust,
Must rest, think positive, house is insured, the structure is quite robust.
Tired limbs but alert brain, need to unwind, induce stillness, try to
let go.
Meditate on tranquil things, breathe deeply, surrender, move with
the flow.
But in solitude, thoughts disturb me, darkness fosters negative
feeling to encase,
Questions spring to mind, worries, problems, multiply at alarming pace.
Why evil, hate, anger, violence, discord, unrest, appear to prevail,
When a phrase shines through, 'Come unto me, all ye who travail.'
This quotation illumes like a beacon, to indicate, assure, direct the way,
Allows me to switch off, float in a stress free bubble, 'sufficient
unto the day'
At the centre of the storm, Christ commanded the tempest, 'Peace,
be still'
A demonstration of mastery over the elements, which bow to
divine will.
Through the power of prayer, healing words console,
neutralise conflict.
Open an avenue of confidence, trust, counsel to inspire and uplift.
Provide a safe haven when life's trials and tests become too demanding,
Construct a sanctuary of faith, hope, love, comfort and understanding.
The road is sometimes difficult, necessitates attention and care,
Anxiety, nervous tension, require conviction to counter, restore
and repair.
Please keep my perspective balanced, to value harmony, good,
kind intent,
To appreciate and treasure, grace and blessings heaven sent.
Thank you for every cheerful, gladdening experience, may I with
charity repay.
Grant inner calm to transcend alarm, your precepts, guidelines to obey.
I appreciate family, friends, pleasures, interests, provision of
daily bread,

Lord, sincere gratitude for warmth, security of home, snugness of
                                                    my bed.
The formation of another dawn, with routine, schedules to
                                            maintain, pursue,
Renewed heart and spirit, energy replenished to shape an
                                            optimistic view.
For nutrients, shelter, stimulus, communication, education,
                                        rewarding sensation
Observation, fascination, participation in the marvel and majesty
                                            of creation.

Dennis Overton

THE PLOUGH AND THE SOWER

The plough lies on its side,
Its blades face sky and earth
Halfway up the field, where the ground rises.
Below it, dark soil lies turned in deep rows
Across the gradient.
Heavy
Rich
Good soil,
Now warmed by the sun.
A blackbird moves among the clods,
Worms are there, food.

Above the plough the field slopes
And billows,
Spattered green with rough grass
Growing through the stubble of
Last year's wheat.
A skylark soars and sings above
The hard soil.

The plough is turned away from the hill.
Its blades are dulled by rain.
The skylark sings undisturbed
Above the rising slope.
The sower turns back.
Only half the field.
It has been like this for weeks.

A L Skevington

ENCOUNTERS

I dreamed you walking in the night and rain
High heeled clicks on paving stone
Sigh of our souls in a soulless age
Eyes alight with things to come.
All that was London sixty-four
When we unfurled our banners
Proclaimed our brave new world
The years before the fall.
I saw you stagger in the autumn leaves
I saw you rummage in the bin
Dead eyed ruin set in trees
Talking to yourself of gin.
I'd heard you whisper in the rain
Never the same we'll be again.

Douglas Macleod

A NIGHT IN NOVEMBER

A sparkle in November -
a crackle and a pop.
Remember oh remember -
gunpowder, treason and plot.

Children jump in merriment
with lanterns burning bright -
a bowl of soup to warm each heart,
on this November night.

The rockets zoom way up high,
a snow storm bursts its cloud -
the Guy Fawke slowly withers and dies
watched by the cheering crowd.

Sparklers twist and turn around
in excited little hands,
a crackling banger makes a sound
like the boom of a big brass band.

There's jacket potatoes roasting on the fire -
bowls of long awaited soup,
a cascade of stars shoot higher and higher
and one little chap's lost his boot.

Now then kiddies - it's time to go,
we'll all come again next year -
back to the house where the fire casts its glow
as we sit in our cosy armchairs . . .

Then - Dad smokes his pipe -
Mother does some knitting
the kiddies play their games
and Granny feeds the kitten.

Wendy Watkin

THE SIXTH SENSE

Sight is the power of witnessing
How others do lead us astray . . .
We are influenced from an early age
And we falsely think, 'This is the way'.

We hear all the ways people argue
Picking faults, even where there are none . . .
And because we are so easily led
We assume this is how it is done . . .

Smell can be a real misconception
An aroma, which seems to be sweet . . .
Is so often just a smoke screen
Concealing some obnoxious deceit . . .

Our taste buds are tempted endlessly
By things which are bad for our health . . .
We're bombarded from every possible source
To increase the producers' wealth . . .

Touch seems the most reassuring
Of the senses, with which we are blessed . . .
But when it's replaced by another's
We are left alone, feeling depressed . . .

The sixth sense, however, is reliable
There's no fallacy, right from the start . . .
That eerie feeling of who you can trust
Seems to come from deep in your heart . . .

Enrico

60'S DREAMING

Something in the air
A sense of sharing
For we were young
And the tale
Had just begun

Songs heard
In the night wind
Moved you so deep
Magical connections
To other worlds

Communal squalor
'Oz' and 'It'
Romantic layabouts
Ironic and knowing
So deep
In the underground:
Long haired girls
Cool and casual
Skinny dipping
Under the moon

And the sadness
When the dream
Went sour
The colours fading
Falling down
To earth again
With such a bump.

Julian Ronay

BIG FOOT

Cold eerie night
Shadows are cast
You're not alone
If you're in the woods tonight
You'll hear him moan.
Blood on his claws
Lone walker of prey
If you're near the woods tonight
Keep well *away.*

Mark Page

I WISH

I wish there was a world where there was no war,
I wish there was a world full of peace and harmony,
A world with no pollution that did not kill animal and marine
life more and more,
A beautiful world with a wonderful ecology,
What wonderful world if this could be a world for all the
future children to live in and see,
But instead we have a world full of war and strife,
A world full of pollution killing all marine and land animal life,
When will the wars and all the polluting stop or is it now too late,
If man acts now he may save all the world's pollution fate,
We need to act right away to try to regain and make the world
as it was before so all life can breathe and live again.

R Muir

DEAR GRANDMA - I KNOW NOW?

(For Olivia Smith, 1922 - 1996)

Dear Grandma - I know now
You don't want me to sit and cry
you want me to be calm
and not think of you all the time
even though it is hard to cope.
You want me to look after my mum
just in case she can't help
but cry for you.
I know this now
and from now on I am going to try!

Victoria Webb

IF WISHES WERE HORSES

If wishes were horses
beggars would surely ride,
to places beyond the blue to find;
a place secure, to hide,
then dwell there in perfect peace,
untouched by earthly care,
and always joyously sing,
of life so rich and fair.

There would I tell,
and its citizens dazzle
with tales of how,
on earth diamonds drizzle,
to enliven the bush and flowers
to blossoms bright,
turning the once dull earth,
into a rainbow of light.

Looks like we are all like beggars,
wishing for horses to ride
and escape these burdens,
our usual lot this side.

But if we are to bear,
and all burdens, gladly share,
we need a song to sing,
as this flight home, we dare;
on a magical 'golden wing'.

George Saurombe

THE FACE OF MILLBURN BEACH (N E SCOTLAND)

Seated on the edge, eyes dark,
Mysteriously gazing out to sea,
In the heat of the day - cold to the touch,
Shadows echo across a blemished facade.
Bristling winds, white horse waves,
A continuous erosion through an age of sea, salt and air,
Majestic pose, a view of worldly satire,
Timeless invasion of man and beast,
Captured - within an entity of stone.
A blue spectrum permeates calm vision; creative dread,
Singing choruses, howling bridges between seasons,
Feet submerged below grinding rocks and brandishing waves,
A giant effigy, monumental head,
Unable to egress the ebb and flow upheld by universal gravity.
Resigned to the sound of laughter, squeals of trepidation,
Children's dare devil games upon its shoulders,
Prickling toes, bravado, strength, climbing hands upon its cheeks,
Triumphant dancing upon its head.
A rock - to many without foresight and vision - calamity endured,
Corrosion grinding away at its innocence,
Eventual submergence to total disdain,
Upon a world of ever changing faces.

Jacqui Buckley

SPACE ADVENTURE

A million miles from havens' safe,
Outward bound for stars far distant
Nothingness beyond your ship,
Engine churns and thrums persistent,
You reach in mind for fantasy's theme,
But, in space, no one can hear you dream.

On routine voyage to who knows where,
Sharing space with cosmic dust
And a few loyal companions
Whose sexless friendship you can trust,
You reach in mind for lover's scheme,
But, in space, no one can hear you dream.

Upwards no longer is direction
And seconds do not measure time.
Space/time continues round a curve.
You eat and drink recycled slime.
Of brave explorers you're the cream,
But, in space, no one can hear you scream.

David W Lankshear

PORTRAIT OF A PAINTER - MONET

The speckles of life in coloured dreams,
were pieced together in painted scenes.
When Claude Monet wet his brush,
people's lives stood, hushed.

Placed up high, spanning the walls.
Framed by brilliance and decorating the halls.
His busy brushes canvassed inside,
away from posing people's pride.

His life began with eyes so clear,
that details brought the spectator near.
But years of colouring and failing sight,
sadly took the seeing light.

So celebrate the legacy,
that dangles from the nail,
and appreciate the price tag at Sotheby's art sale!

Kim Taylor

PARADISE NOT FORGOTTEN

They twirled, floated, danced and shimmered, the motes upon the
                                                    beam of sunlight.
Above me a soft green canopy of gently twisting leaves in
                                                    southern breeze.
Shafts of light drifted from the harebell blue flecks of the silken sky.
Not a puff of cotton wool cloud to mar its surface.
I lay amongst cool sweet smelling grass and soft furry moss, as
                                                    comfy as a feather bed.
A fluttering and buzzing of wings and hurrying, scurrying,
                                                    crawling insects,
Who are going about their business within the grass around me.
Floating fragrances from a myriad herbs and gaily coloured flowers.
Drifting in and out of semi-consciousness, my worries and
                                                    troubles shrink away.
Heaven sent peace and tranquillity.
This is my paradise to return to in memory when winter once
                                                    more presents itself.

I S Hinton

TO BE

A gypsy on the seashore
Walked down to the sea
Pulled towards the blue
And the taste of salt
Sparks of fire
Magic in her eyes
She soared high above
The seagulls' cries
The wind tugged at her hair
Her swirling clothes
Were never as gusty as she.
And splintered lights
Played upon the waves
A puffin motionless upon a rock.
Sky, grey and electric
I longed to come here
She spoke
You are here
Spoke the sea . . .

Vanessa Cranmer

GRADUATION

Faked pomp, fanfare and procession,
solemn cap-and-gown masquerade,
pretended lineage.

Students stacked high in rows,
like cans on supermarket shelves
waiting in purgatory to be called.
Flamboyant body art tidied away
uniformly tamed by academic gowns
EEC stamped, sized and graded
as graduating sausages.

But at the edge of the dias
where most pray not to trip,
or nervously finger wobbly mortar board,
one tall black girl theatrically casts off her gown
and underneath a tight leather mini-dress
is sprayed onto her body.
She strides onto the stage, ignoring dignitaries,
- a hush - anticipation - stewards tense -
she raises up long arms and parts her feet
stamping a great black X against the academics
and slowly executes two perfect cartwheels
across the space where others nod obsequiously
arm and leg spokes suspended in the air
a V to the establishment
a V for victory.

Maggie Butt

THE GARBAGE MAN

If I was a bin man,
　　I'd travel all the roads,
Collecting people's garbage,
　　By bag or by the load.
I'd sort out all the useful bits,
　　Before incineration,
Even people's cast off clothes,
　　I'd give consideration.
The broken toys, I'd take back home,
　　And mend for girls and boys,
Who have no mum and dad,
　　To buy them such nice toys.
The cast off clothes, as you suppose,
　　I'd take home to my wife.
With her machine she'd sew the seams,
　　And give the clothes new life.
We'd give the clothes to poorer folk,
　　Who have no clothes to wear,
Or people who are out of work,
　　Without a dime to spare.
You see, though not a bin man,
　　I also have a dream,
To do a job, and help all folk,
　　And keep the country clean.
The next time, when out for a walk,
　　There's litter on the ground,
Pick it up, put in the bin,
　　You'll find my logic sound.

Lionel J Nokes

DENIAL

I don't wanna
understand the horrors of the world
I don't wanna
see the blood on your hands
I don't wanna
see the name tags on toes
I don't wanna
hear the screams inside your head
I don't wanna
except the truth in your eyes
I don't wanna
know what's really happening
I just wanna
believe your soften lies.

Susan Rae Nott

CIRCULAR TOUR

Something is missing, it had an abyss in
It is lying there prone in that bowl
It is less than it should be, more of it would suit me
I like it much better when all of it is whole
It does not look wholesome - someone has stole some
It is something that looks out of this world
Tell me completely why is something that acts sweetly
So deformed - I do need the reason unfurled
What about its formation - it is such a small ration
Much less than it rightly should be
Tell me my dearest - about the one that is nearest
I need to clear up this strange mystery
It seems somewhat less truthful in that bowl that is near full
Please tell me - I promise I won't tell a soul
It looks really quite quaint dear, I am scared of it, I do fear
It is the first time I have seen - a doughnut with a hole!

John L Wright

LIFE

Sitting, at the sidewalk table,
Watching, the people go by,
Funny faces everywhere,
Making us smile, fancy shoes,
Where, you get, those mules.

Interrogation, irritation,
Manhole covers, irrigation.

Plain white paper, illustrations,
Lucid thoughts, no hesitation.
Fancy cars, fumigation.
Long cold glances, abrogation.

Spaghetti hoops, liposuction.
Plastic macs, infiltration.
Sudden jolts, x-ray vision.
Fancy hat, no illusions.

Red leather jackets, improvisation,
Scanty clouds, humanisation.
Mannerism's gone,
Long white faces.

Red deer passing, fascination,
Umberto's calling, generalisation.
Long white trousers, sensitive teeth,
Governmental departments, are
All these things, detrimental.

Terry Ramanouski

INGRATITUDE

Hens are now required
To batter out their eggs;
Not asked whether they are tired
They have got to do their best
With their eggs to feed
The mind and body of man's greed.
Why not say, 'Thank you'
For each egg the hen has laid.
She may in her sheer gratitude
Lay many more eggs instead.

Can you not see how you err?
The time has come when
You should thank your creator, sir,
That you are not a hen.

M MacDonald-Murray

WHEEL OF THE SUN KING
(Silver circle)

Great grey gracefulness,
wings across the sky,
companion for the male deity,
she flies to accompany and edify.

A goddess metamorphosed,
as a heron, restrained and posed,
all ascetic and parsimonious,
pledges to keep the land harmonious.

To catch fish and place them in a ring,
in honour to Dyonysious the king,
riding on the bull,
she is camouflaged and beautiful.

As harbinger, she transformed to vessel,
of treasures; hallows and many a spell,
until the old religion faded,
forgotten mostly, and degraded.

Fallen to low estate and superstition,
certain priests saw no volition,
of hags in their graves before ripe time,
but saw that as a crime.

Soon now, the veil shall be lifted,
to reveal the gnosis to the gifted,
and restore the taboo back to the sacred,
when certain virtues are wed.

And as ancient laws revitalise
these things again will be seen
amongst the wise,
to rise in esteem.

In the efficacy of equilibrium,
within the eternal continuum,
the silver circle will shine
light, upon all things divine.

Ariadne

LIVING THE WAY

If we only sought to weather
All our weather and our clime.
If we only bore the bother
Of our brothers' beneficial time.
We should find our pathway brighten
On the passage of our way,
We should feel our burdens lighten
And progress through prospects grey.
If we only caught the message
As proclaimed in gospels four.
If we only made the best age
Alive now and ever more.
We should fill the world with gladness,
We should spread pure love and joy,
We should grow to glory endless
Bear rich fruit and faith employ.
We should hear angelic voices
All around us day and night.
We should know our righteous choices
Build a heaven of beauty bright.

David W Hill

SWEET DREAM

(After Baudelaire)

Greedy, indeed, in voluptuous headiness,
Have you never inhaled the powerful bouquet
Of a grain of incense percolating through a church,
Breathed in the potency of musk in a sachet?

Mysterious necromancy by which the resurrected past
Conjures the here and now, the eternal present.
Thus the lover gathers up the exquisite flower
Of memory from his beloved's body's scent,

From the potent, palpable sachet gathers it up -
Her censer of heavy, coiled, cascading hair, beauty
From which the wild musk rises up,

As from her fabrics - silk, velvet, muslin -
Each permeated with her youthful purity,
There emanates the perfume of her skin.

Norman Bissett

THE VILLAGE

In my silent worlds of thought
I look on villages trapped or caught
By words and beauty beyond all man
Where I escape to when I can
And sit in silence to meet my mind
With valued rapture of the kind
That leaves me underneath a tree
Loving the landscape's simplicity
Or wander down the remembered path
By the canal where a presence hath
Flown delighting in a day from school
Where we ran and joked and forgot the rule
That binds young people to their tasks
Because that day in sunshine basked
And kicked the nettles and took delight
In making stories that just might
Be looked upon half believingly
And sent an impish spirit jumping free
Such days escape the inner content
And rove in the clouds of innocence
That I view and behold and lead
To reach me in ecstasies within the breeze
A lovely breeze on a summer's day
That I take to my heart and am led away
In villages and things beyond
Everyday man and his common song
To play football and revel in
A trick with footwork that can
beat that mid-field then a clear pass
Such joy in an open field of grass
Or at an older age, the village pub
The real ale and smell of grub
While yonder church chimes merrily
Such is the delight of village life to me
Mundane life has pulled me down

And disciplined me in its common ground
Money swears and I now believe
In modern pain, that's to be relieved
Only by more money for drink and travelling
To release the hours and pain they would bring
The village life shall be my target
Forget the fast food, the television and the hyper-market
The way of life of modern concrete
That alienates and distances the grass from your feet
Live for the church, the railway and dream
Of a summer's day of contentment in the old village green
Slow down the pace of the world's modern pain
Let the village set you free again and again.

Mike Fuller

RESTRICTED

'I'm sorry you can't come in here,
We just haven't got the room,
This restaurant is far too small,
We'd fall over you in the gloom'.

Oh dear, you can't get in there,
The steps are far too high,
The library is not the place for you,
Give WHSmith's a try.

I'll go and see a film instead,
They are showing 'Alien Nations',
'I'm sorry Sir, you can't come in,
It's against fire regulations'.

That's it, I'm going to the pub,
To forget my cares and woes,
I can't get in, the door's too small,
But that's the way life goes.

Especially for me, I can't walk you see,
So I have to use this wheelchair,
So many places I can't go,
It really fills me with despair.

So what do I do? I stay at home,
Then you never have to change,
You can just pretend I don't exist,
Or that my needs are strange.

But heaven help it should happen to you,
Then you would understand the pain,
Of being treated as second class,
Again and again and again.

S M Hooper

LIFE'S WAYS

Life is the thing that we are in,
Life decides if you're fat or thin,
Life's worth living, yes it is,
It's the new Michael Jackson, it is the biz.

Animals have lives too,
Lives are not just for me and you,
The animals eat and drink and sleep,
And these lives we hope to keep.

We live in life and life we live,
We like to have fun and still we give,
Out other feelings all the time,
But we still keep living and feeling fine,

In our sleep you might not think,
That we will grow and we will sink,
But after all we do all change,
And lots of things are very strange,

Do you ever wonder why,
We should give up when tension's high?
But still we live with things we hate,
And life can be a heavy weight.

Well when life's up like a game over,
You leave your friends and your dog Rover,
So you can now just wait and see,
How good your lives can really be.

Claire Tidey

BY YOUR OWN HAND

For months afterwards,
if I held the door at a certain angle,
I could see you
in the tumble drier.

While it made a change
from finding your face
in leaves and feathers,
I felt you watch me
work through the dirty linen
that marked your death.

I thought of how
we'd shared the same womb
and wondered if you'd left it clean
for my beginning
or if traces of you
could be found in me.

Spring came
and you had long left your glassy frame.
Instead, you came to me at night,
your thin artist's hands extended
and I reached out
in joy that you had found me

but looking down,
I saw the dirt thickened
under your nails
and knew, then,
the sin was yours.

Awakened,
I searched the house for your hands
and found them hanging
in oils
which slid
too easily into the trash.

It is winter now,
and I long for lost images.

A P Rollins

SHOPPED

The weather being good
Requiring some food
Off I went shopping
For items wanting.

Arriving home by taxi
What did I see?
We both glared
As tho' snared.

I sat frowned
Feeling spellbound
Could hardly believe
My eye did see

A board some fool
Had nailed to the wall
My bungalow 'for sale'
An absurd confused tale

As I surveyed
My memory did fade
Was this a 'yoke'
From some folk

If I was being teased
One was displeased
With all my wits
I phoned the culprits

To them I did refer
Saying 'joke over'
Without any fuss
Simply told 'wrong house'

Josephine Foreman

LAMENT

She's gone now;
a pall hangs over Bryn Caerffili;
black was her hair,
black like the crow on the stone of her grave;
brown were her eyes,
brown like the wren on the banks of the Tâf;
soft were her cheeks,
soft like the wool on the lambs of Eglwysilan;
warm was her smile,
warm like the primrose in the woods of Efailisaf;
sweet were her lips,
sweet like the waters of Nangarw;
music was her voice,
music like children's voices on the Graigwen air;
brightly shone her soul,
bright like the cross on the altar of Capel Rhondda;
endless were my tears,
endless like the waves on Barri sands;
broken was my heart,
a pall hangs over the Garth,
she's gone now.

Ted Spanswick

REDUNDANCY FROM THE CHILDREN'S HOME

There once was a lady called Christine
Who cycled to work each day
She battled through all of the elements
So she could earn a day's pay.

On arrival at Westdene at 8.30
She parked her bike in its usual spot
She hung up her coat on the coat peg
And proceeded to get out her mop
Up the staircase she would then go
To the Grenfell Unit that she did know
Into the bedrooms, kitchen and lounge,
Hoovering everything up that she found
With sweeping strokes and duster at hand
She left the place just looking grand.

At approximately 10.45 the coffee bell rang
And Christine would join the rest of the gang
A cup of coffee, a biscuit or two, catch up on the goss
It gets you through!

On with the work, always willing to help
Christine got everything done and under her belt
Off on her bike at 12.30 sharp better get home before it's dark.

Tomorrow would come and she'd do the same thing
But alas the day came when redundancy set in
Christine was out along with the rest
After all the years of giving her best.

She was soon on the hunt, a new job to find
Filling in application forms, time after time.
Success of interview soon came and now she is gone
I wonder how we will now get along?

We will miss her smile and banter each day
But in our hearts she will always stay
We'll keep in touch no fear of that
Still find time for coffee and chat
Good Luck Christine in all you do
We will never forget you.

June Slater

THE NEARLY MAN

Would born with a silver spoon
    Have broadened my horizons
Or ambition fed
    Brought on stress
To start a chain reaction.
    Might I have been a statesman
Believing in my spin
    Or courting sleaze and vice
To bridge the gap between.
    If I had reached the pinnacle
As a novel writer
    Would I have slipped
Lost my grip
    My name changed to a number.
Creativity by connection
    Put in the spotlight
Millionaire or weakest link
    No doubt would find me out.
As a sporting personality
    In the public eye
My nature leans to Jack the lad
    Not training with desire.
If the ladies in my life
    Had belonged to upper crust
Would conversation, imagination
    Strain to bit of rough.
On reflection these words
    Have shown me in new light
A nearly man in limbo
    Paranoid of great divide.

Robert Fallon

CLOCKWORK HEART

Wind up your clockwork heart
Put on your clockwork shoes
If you don't hurry you'll be late
To blow your clockwork fuse!
I watch you rushing off to town
The same time every morning
Like lemmings to the underground
All blurry eyed and yawning
All crammed together face to face
Infirmed, inflamed and afflicted
Reality is running rife!
Just as they predicted
I watch you trying not to breathe
Afraid of conversation
Inhaling till you're fit to bust
And exploding on the station
So wind up your clockwork heart
Put on your clockwork shoes
If you don't hurry you'll be late
To blow your clockwork fuse!

Rod Trott

HOW FASHIONS CHANGE!

In days of old, women were bold;
Then they did not wear leather,
But sticks and stones, with bits of string
To tie the lot together.

Some women said these were too hard,
And so a man called Bert
Became a dress designer,
And made the first grass skirt.

The women still weren't satisfied -
This grass was home to moths;
So Bert then made another skirt
From something he called cloth.

But, sad to say, the moths preferred
This cloth much more than grass;
Which left Bert tearing out his hair,
And moaning, 'Oh, alas!'

At last, in desperation,
He made skirts of something tinny;
He made a short one for his wife
That's why he called it Minnie!

Since then fashions have altered,
Both in country-wear and town;
And skirts behave like yo-yos,
As their hems go up and down!

Roger Williams

SHE

The doctor came on and he told me she had died.
She and me stopped for a moment,
Smiled at one another and carried on
With what we were doing;

Me reading beside her,
Her washing the walls of her hospital bed.

It was spring as I walked home
To where she was waiting with
Charts and plans for cleaning,

Exactly as she does every spring.

Peter Asher

UNTITLED

At night I only see white.
It is my canvas.
I'm not afraid of the dark.
I'm a big lad, you see.
If others are afraid,
I try not to be.
If they can get you in the dark,
They can get you during the day.
I paint at night
Because it's white.
My body sleeps, but I am free.

Gregory Santo Arena

CHILD OF CHRISTMAS

I wish the ghosts of Christmas, would knock upon my door,
To bring me Christmas spirit, like I knew long before.
When I believed in Christmas, Santa Claus and all,
The tinsel and the fairy lights, the Christmas tree, each ball.

My heart just feels so empty no signs of Christmas there,
And I have searched so long and hard it really feels unfair.
Santa doesn't visit, no present 'neath the tree,
Perhaps that's why my spirit's gone, and the spirit must see me.

I listen for my clock to chime, twelve, then one, then two,
No spirits visit me like Scrooge, and now the night's half through.
I curl up on my window sill, to scan the rooftops high,
In hope I see the bearded one, with reindeer in the sky.

The frosty night it sparkles, no single sign of snow,
And time is just a ticking, going by so slow.
I climb down from my window, and curl up in my bed,
And pray the Christmas spirit, will fill my heart and head.

Then my door bursts open, 'Daddy Santa's been,'
And then I find the Christmas spirit, more than I have seen.
Her eyes they sparkle brightly, so much more than snow,
Her face it fills my heart with joy, the spirit's here I know.

And as we dig beneath the tree, I hark her squeals of joy,
As wrapping paper flies around, revealing every toy.
And as we sit amongst the toys, one present left to go,
Who's the present for we ask? No label, we don't know.

And as the present's opened, a gift to one and all,
Within a manger lies a child, curled up in a ball.
The ghost of Christmas came to me, the child completed me,
That year I found my Christmas cheer, wrapped up beneath my tree.

Geoffrey Woodhead

THE LANE

The lane I knew when I was a child,
was spooky with trees that would hang right down.
There were beech trees, horse chestnut trees
and one old walnut tree as well.
What a lovely mess they would make in autumn time
when all the nuts would fall on the ground.
There were birds in the hedgerows,
chirping away creating a signal
that would scare the rabbits away.
There were cows in the meadow munching the grass
and we would stop and lean on the field gate
as we passed.
But now, alas, it is all gone, even the lane.
What is left there to be seen,
houses and roads, cars whistling past.
People who live there will never know
that once long ago
it was just a leafy, spooky lane.

Kay O'Connell

TOMORROW'S REVIEW

I stepped amongst reminders
Of more exotic days
Walked a brambled footpath
Once well trod
Gazed through a roof
To the mackerel sky,
At a door that leaned
From its hinge nearby
In a dockland bleak and grey
Relics of the golden years
Silenced where they lay
Victims of progress
Change and decay,

Moored at the Quayside
Beyond the foxgloves
A modern tanker gleamed
In the sunlit morn
Her mooring ropes dangling, untried
Her busy pumps replenishing
The dormant lifeline
Of industry, no less
A symbol of hope
In the wilderness.

Jack Pritchard

BEAUTY

Around the circlet the halo
Of the gold and jewels
Reduplicated and echoed
Chic and stylish the cotton velvet
Gathered fulgent fribbles
In dignity
Stitchery frontal and frou frou
Appreciably
Apprehensible
Conventionally
Trifles with the stephanotis

Citronella yielding the
Circum
The tenzon
In step
Statuesquely
Is
Perceptible
The ponderable fable
Chiaroscuro
Like a chameleon
Contributing to
The transverse.

Straight-forwardly
Straight away
The marvellous tale
Bands
Sums up
The suffix
Transversely
Conversely
Gathers.

The inflexion
Grammatical ally
In context

Contributes
And
Contrives
To make an
Apologue
The stratus refluent
On
In step
Applys
A
Conjugation
Frequentative
And
Fuluous.

Sarah Margaret Munro

THE SECRET

I know a secret but I cannot tell,
For if I do, it might spell,
The end of the magic in the dell,
Rustling leaves, a tinkling bell,
Have you guessed? It's hard to tell,
A ring, a toadstool in the fell,
I know a secret, do you know now as well?

S Grebby

COURTNEY

A little Courtney person with a smiley two teeth grin,
Charged across the room and banged her head against my shin.
She banged her head against the table, and then against the wall,
Then smiling with a two teeth grin, said, 'It didn't hurt at all.'

A little Courtney person with a grin so big and wide,
Was sitting on the settee, quietly by my side.
She did a double somersault and then began to sing,
'I landed upside down but I never felt a thing.'

A little Courtney person pulled by CDs from the rack,
Pressed the buttons on the radio and knocked my record off its track.
She gave a toothy grin and spoke, though I couldn't understand,
'I didn't mind the vocals, but I didn't like the band.'

A little Courtney person has subjects to discuss,
And if no one will listen she starts to make a fuss.
She has views on everything, that adults have to say,
But when she finds us boring she will simply go and play.

A little Courtney person seems to know an awful lot,
I don't know where she learned it, cos she's just a little tot,
But you can ask her almost anything and she'll talk and talk and talk,
I bet it won't be long before she can even walk.

Well she is only 9 months old.

Grandad Sid Haygreen

ONLY YESTERDAYS

I tried to trace the beginnings of all this madness;
sweat pouring off my brow:-

I groped in every closet, every dark corner of my mind:
nothing but cobwebs could I find!

Terrified!
Fingers sweating, groping, blinding,
smashing my way through the decay, silent, silence! Stony silence!

Good God! Where is it? Where is my past?

Thousands of hysterical, laughing voices, looming out of their graves!
But, they have no faces! Oh God, where are their faces?

Is nothing real? I catch up to myself; frantic, afraid, reeling, escape,
yes!

I must escape from myself, oh God, where to?

There is only yesterday. Ah! Ah! Ah! Only yesterday
Only a million light years gone by,
I pulled the curtains across from the screen!
Nothing there.

Nothing but the stark smell of dead remorse.

Tomorrow never came, did it John?
You were always caught up, in heavy dreams of a futile tomorrow.
A tomorrow that could never be.

Living, heart-beating, sweating, running from a dark past,
it won't leave me alone!

Now I know my jailer, my oppressors, they are the anvil weighted
memories; the roots; 'my roots'- my past!

I can't get away from the truth!

The nightmares, the blind tears - they are, irrevocable past!

On, and then my dear boy John, on and on, until all of your past work is done!

Aye, until all is done.

John Gaze

STALEMATE
(Respectfully dedicated to both sides of the family)

'These are all very tough negotiations,'
Correctly insisted the supervisor.
'For they are only going to become tougher
With the passing of time itself,'
His deputy still respectfully reminded him.
'But only if we unconditionally surrender ourselves,
And our desires,'
His superior had cautiously spoken his mind,
Only to be challenged further with
This requisite objective:-
'We must always ensure that this certainly does not happen again.'
- For the abject veracity of his comment itself,
Distinctly overrode the already now inevitable consequences
Of his admirably forthcoming remark.
'Nothing and no one must now stop us.
We should, at all costs, purposely avoid
The downright unreasonable position
Of complete stalemate,
Both now and indeed, forever more.'

Michael Denholme Hortus Stalker

THE MORNING DANCE

Flowers at the morning dance
Who scent the wind's cool breath
As they drink the heady nectar of the dew
Still each and every dawn enhance
And, though you are in death, my sweet
They'll always remind me of you.

Kim Montia

NIGHT AND THE CITY

Neons
blinking on/off . . .
At The Pink Flamingo
alcohol drowns the loneliness . . .
sometimes.

Good time
gals, dames and dolls
mooching the sidewalks; all
cigarette smoke, high heels and bright
lipstick.

Mitchum
walking the night
in a trench coat and hat,
keeping the shadows company
till dawn.

Widmark
on the hustle;
all sneering villainy
picking up kisses of death on
South Street.

Ryan
at RKO;
tough, nocturnal iceman
turning up the heat in LA
No sweat.

Fast trains
piercing the night
from city to city
carrying hopes and dreams through the
darkness.

Cavan Magner

END OF AN ERA

'Twas the final demonstration, of the miners power
And frustration, dealing with the iron maiden
Claws of tempered steel unladen.

Thousands and thousands of people
Assembled in Hyde Park, it was a sight to see
Men, women and children, from every part of the country.

Now at last they moved off, bands began to play
Pipes, drums, tin whistles, the order of the day.

A line of policemen here, a line of policemen there
Each time they glanced to take a look
There were policemen everywhere.

They finally reached Trafalgar Square
A great hue and cry it did ring out
The men from Wales were not seen about.

But, they could see it was sheer bedlam back there
Placards and policemen's helmets
Flying through the air.

'Move one step forward,' this policeman did say
'And you are arrested, on this very day.'

I still cannot forget that memorable day
Nineteen seventy-six, February not May.

The end of an era, sad but true
The miners were beaten
The Unions too.

James Loughran

A LETTER TO MY FAMILY TREE

If you are reading this letter it's because I've passed away
It's not because I've left you, it's God's wish that this be my day.
You must remember always you are always a part of me.
And that I will always love you, I'm part of your family tree.
Remember what I taught you, the difference between right and wrong
And I will be happy in Heaven singing a happy song.
You all represent me in my absence and carry on my cause
I will be right behind you all to hear each and every applause.
Don't ever think you hurt me even though at times words are said
There are always bad times, but think of the goods ones instead.
Love is the strongest word and the greatest word we possess.
A man is strong who possesses love but one without is weak
                                       and oppressed.
I will always be with you all to the end of time for sure
Because we are all a part of God's world that He wanted to be so pure.
Respect everything and everyone for this you will be blessed.
I'm so proud of each and all of you and wish you each success
I will be here watching over you, so don't you become depressed.
You only have one shot at life, so grab it by the hand
All your clocks are ticking, so enjoy it, don't hang around.
And that I will never ever die because you are a part of me
So when you're feeling lonely look in the mirror and see
That I will never leave you, because in yourself you will see me.

Irene Smith

DAD'S GROWMORE MIXTURE

Me dad had an allotment, by the river Irk,
Where he would tend his cabbages, when he'd finished work.
He'd carrots big as forearms, and taters big as clogs
And sprouts that grew like trees, and were weed on by the dogs.
There was a marrow like a barge, supported by a plank
And an onion like a turret, upon a Churchill tank.
We'd always food aplenty - and our neighbours too
For Dad was very generous, with all the food he grew.
His secret was quite simple - his method quite unique
He got old hops from the brewery, and every other week
he would put them in the rain barrel, and, then every day
He'd feed this 'mixture' to his plants, in such a loving way.
The hops would be mixed to the soil upon his plot
And Dad would often say - 'That soil has got the lot.'
The men on the allotments, knew nothing of his ways
They would peep into his garden and enviously gaze
But pride would not allow them, to ever ask my dad
Why his plants grew so big - and made their own look sad.
Dad was quite a joker, and on his plot one day
With a wink to his mate, he was loudly heard to say
'Just in case owt 'appens, I'd like Thee to 'ave me plot
Look after all me plants with love - tha can 'ave the lot.'
'But how do thou manage' says his mate, 'to grow to such a size?'
'Cos I empty t'chamber on 'em all,' with a twinkle in his eyes.
Well all those gardeners scurried home, and grabbed a chamber pot
And every day upon their plants, they emptied out the lot.
This ritual was followed, each day throughout the year
And while their plants smelled of wee - Dad's all smelled of beer.
The place has changed o'er the years - it caused such a row
Where once grew finest plants, there is a cesspit now.

John Burton

EMPTY HOUSE

A small stone house on a hill
Stands so silent 'stands' so still.
Not a sound remains there
Only the creaking of a mouse on the stair.
Only the wind visits and passes through
Through the house, I once shared with you.
So happy we were together, together alone
In our lovely house, a happy home.
But now, you are gone,
To Heaven, high up above,
All that is left is our house
And my undying love.
Our house stands empty for all to see,
But it can never be so empty
As losing you left me.

Trudie Sullivan

A SLICE OF HUMANITY

Melting in the pot of years,
A million smiles, a million tears,
Stirred with a froth of joy, restrained
By a torrent of tears of pain.
Mountains of spice, folded with care,
A treasure here, some beauty there,
A hug of friends, some fools lament
Sprinkled with wisps of sentiment.
A snip of dreams, a blend of rhyme,
Whisked by the endless winds of time.
Some shakes of terror, a quiver of fear,
A thunder of laughter tinged with tears.
Season with destiny, small pinch of fate,
With a handful of luck and a soupçon of hate,
One quick squeeze of jealousy, barrels of love,
Leavened by sanity, hope from above.
Knead with humility, baste with urbanity,
Top with a crust of humour and vanity,
Mould with concern, bake in tranquillity,
Serve for a lifetime - a slice of humanity.

C D Isherwood

THE YOUNG SLAVE GIRL'S SONG BY A STREAM

Lucent water, so silver, clear;
What dreaded terror
do thy depths fear?

Feel not my tears (surface thin).
Thou feel not care:
No soul within.

No anguish seem, (thy ripples chase),
So swiftly flowing,
sees not my face.

Thou doth dance: (with gleams rejoice),
Sing of freedom!
Thou purest voice.

Could I ever frisk as Thee?
I have a mistress
who rules of me.

Dorothy Mary Allchin

BILLY BUTTON

Just last week upon the stair I heard a noise but there was no one
there. I heard it again just the other day, I wish that someone would
find somewhere else to play.

Well whatever happened to my outside loo, going up and down these
stairs could be the death of me. Well I know you can't see me, but
the someone on your stairs is really me, Billy Button.

And what's this I hear about your Christmas tree, is there
someone shaking it, well it's me! I shake it just to see if there's a
surprise present just for me.

But every year is always the same, and I know you're really not to
blame. So just for a change I would like to see a neatly wrapped
present just for me, Billy Button.

Thanks for letting me share this cottage with you, as so many others
have had to do. You see I'll still be here long after you've gone, so I
promise I won't do anything wrong. I'll see you soon, but I doubt that
you'll see me, once heard, never forgotten, Billy Button.

Robert Waggitt

ME AND HORSES

Mares in ever movement in a sheltering and a shielding,
The newly born foals, lying still as if were dead.
Suddenly surprises their earnest mums by flying off in a frenzied
dance, all wobbly legs, with head and tail afleeting.
The young of last year adorn the next field, all seven beauties
The whites, the greys and blacks and reds, all sporting white
                                                    ankle socks.
Its cheeky now they be showing a full mouth of teeth as in a
grin, whilst pushing my hand off his pinkish nose.
Exquisite to the tongue clicking sound, or sound of ring to gate.
Could food be near, not from this strange person on two wheels
This splendid noble creature, who intermingles with the sheared
sheep and their little lambs and shares the flowing streams as the
great beeches and the stalwart foxgloves are all on guard.
I can be only in Wales.

Margaret Gleeson Spanos

WEDNESDAY, MAY 2ND 2001

There's no chance that I'll forget that date,
When beloved Sweep meandered through the gate,
Which was left open as she didn't roam,
Preferring the security near home.

Now Sweep is old and almost blind, you see,
And loved as much as any dog could be.
She's disabled too, with a failing heart
I dread the day when we finally part.

I just had to find my blue roan.
She shouldn't be afraid and alone.
I feared that she'd come to some harm,
My whole being froze with alarm.

There was no time to waste before it went dark.
As I strained my ears hoping to hear a bark.
I feverishly searched the area around,
My eyes peered intently over every piece of ground.

There were several people passing by
Who were sympathetic, agreeing to try
To find my lost Sweep, feeling sorry for me.
They understood well why she shouldn't be free.

Then I met Diane who went out of her way
With help and support I can never repay.
It was significant that, as she came down the drive,
Sweep returned simultaneously, soaking wet, but alive.

Ina J Harrington

THE BEACONS SLAUGHTER

The mountains bring forth!
Bring forth their living
White creatures.
They stream as a flowing, frothy river,
Flocking from green pastures
To dead ground.

They jostle to their end,
Innocents, once bounding
Across the hills.
Now they fall to the valley
Of the shadow of death.
Following, following, following!
Sheep to the slaughter.
May their funeral pyres
Breathe out the incense
Of their sacrifice!

Nature grieves . . .
She cries out in heaviness.
Her emptiness clothes the mountains.
Sweating blood, stripped naked, whipped,
They stand in silence.
May they be replenished,
Filled, lush once more.
Oh, precious lambs,
Without blemish or spot
May you frolic again,
At home
In the breeze of the mountains.

Judith Thomas

UNTITLED

Looking back
At romantic
Places
In my mind
With all those
Faces
I get a
Feeling deep
Down inside
Most appealing
That I cannot
Hide
Looking back
At romantic
Places
Remember
Them well
With all those
Faces.

Philip Allen

LOVE

I worship the way your mouth moves,
Flows with feeling of love for me.
Affection through your heart's desire,
To take what is your life's desire,
What you adore in life most,
Is passion lurking around the corner?
Waiting for your love's first kiss,
To come at you with care and concern,
Not just a kiss but love,
That longs to last,
Until your life has past.

Ursula Warren

A MIND TO KISS

Before ever we loved
I'd loved forever before.
Before ever we knew
I'd known forever
And more.
Before ever we kissed
I'd a thousand times
Kissed you but then,
To kiss you that first time
Was to kiss you
As never again.

Roger Mosedale

FOOTPRINTS IN THE SAND

When first I held your hand
you left an impression on me
like footprints in the sand

Your kisses, sweet as nectar
make me warm like the day
when first I held your hand

Your gentle caress
remains with me
like footprints in the sand

As we grow old together
the spark is just the same as
when first I held your hand

Your heart is always mine
and my love for you won't crumble
like footprints in the sand

Love's tide is out
but can't wash away the memories of
when first I held your hand,
like footprints in the sand.

Simon Hobson

MARRIAGE

Marriage is when a man takes a wife.
Usually it does mean for life,
You work together to have a home,
To which you welcome family and friends to come by phone.
You have to work at it hard, and save,
For furniture and carpets to be laid.
United together you must be,
Then happy you'll be eternally.
If all goes as it should and when,
Along will come children then
Which will bring you both much joy
Whether the first be a girl or a boy.
Without children it can't be the same,
And I suppose then marriage could become tame.

Pamela Earl

My English Rose

I've looked into those warm, brown eyes
and low and behold the light of Heaven shines
of a crystal clear clarity.
I cannot convey how I feel about you upon this auspicious day.
Your eyes meet mine with that twinkle, that shine.
Smiles all the while a knowing glance, a blissful wink
what this means certainly makes me think.
Falling forever falling for you in many ways what you say, what you do
I may deny it but it's so true.
Oh yes, I'm falling deeply in love with you
I'll love you more today than I did yesterday
my love for you gets stronger day by day
my eternal English rose life is returning to you
as your petals unfold every fragile petal emotionally is worth
                                        its weight in gold.
We all laugh, we all cry, but it's you I want to be with until the day I die
But love, does it ever die, will you, will I?

Jonathan Covington

A POEM OF LOVE

(Dedicated to James Green)

I need to think of you all the time
I can't believe you're actually mine.
This is like a dream come true
I really truly do love you.
You came into my life when I was 'dead'
But I'm happy all the time now instead,
The only problem with the situation is
The fact I cannot live without your kiss.
I'm so pleased that we are now one
When I'm with you I have so much fun.
This is the happiest I've ever been
And you're the most beautiful thing I've ever seen.
I can't wait until I next see you
So that I can show you how much I really love you.
I'd shower you with a million kisses
And show how much you I am missing
I'd have to hug you, and never let go
Because if I did I'd be full of woe.
I would be so sad if I didn't have you
I'd miss all the cheeky little things that you do.
I'm really glad that you're with me
I can't believe I am this happy.

Jodie McKane

ETERNAL LOVE

The first day that I met you,
I thought we'd never part,
The feelings that I felt that day,
Are still here in my heart.
But now you have another guy,
It was for you to choose,
You can't have two, one has to win,
The other has to lose.
O dearest one, how shall I live
Without you by my side?
It's true to say, I thought one day
That you would be my bride.
Though things are not the same now,
I still cannot forget,
The way you looked and smiled at me
The first day that we met.
I can't forget the love I felt
When I held you in my arms,
For I was so in love with you
And smitten by your charms.
But there's one consolation,
I'll always be your friend,
And if you ever need me,
I'll be there to the end.
My love goes on forever,
It does not fade away,
I know somehow, sometime, some place,
I'll be with you some day.
And if we get to Heaven
I'll be with you once more,
I'll hold your hand, just as I planned,
Upon that sunny shore.

James Stanley

MY LOVE

When will I see you again
To tell you I love you
So we can start all over again.

I miss your smiling face
And your laughter oh so loud
When will I see you again?

My love for you will never die
Please pass this way
So we can start all over again.

We would walk in the park
And you would lark around
When will I see you again?

Don't say it's all in vain
As I have walked in the rain
So we can start all over again.

I've loved and lost you
Oh how I miss you
When will I see you again
So we can start all over again?

E Bevans

THE DANCE

As I was walking home one night,
my eyes beheld an eerie sight.
A dark man standing straight and tall
beside the graveyard's stony wall.

'Come - dance with me,' I heard him say,
his voice familiar, but far away.
I knew this man! How could this be?
Tears filled my eyes. I could not see.

The years together had gone so fast.
Twelve months ago my dear one past.
Away to where I could not follow.
My days and nights now cold and hollow.

From echoes lost his sweet voice came,
like angels singing, he called my name.
'Let's play beneath the velvet night,
the moon is full, the stars are bright.'

As in a trance, my mind in shock,
he led me down the churchyard walk.
I heard the sound of music playing.
'Don't let me wake,' my heart was praying.

I felt his hand slip into mine.
We swayed as one, through endless time.
Locked in his arms - a sweet embrace,
I saw once more my loved one's face.

In the gentle dawning's light
As he began to fade from sight,
I heard him whisper in my ear,
'I will return - I'll meet you here.

We'll dance until the day you're laid
beside me in my lonely grave.
Goodbye my love. Don't shed a tear.
Just call my name - I'm always near.'

Polly Davies

FIRST NIGHT

That magic night I can't forget
We danced the night away
We were both so happy and
It could have stayed that way.

But I'm the one who doubted
I couldn't make that call
I now know that I sacrificed
The most cherished love of all.

I really couldn't bring myself
To be the other woman
I lost you, I realise
Because I was so stubborn.

But life was so different then
And marriage was more sacred
It was always frowned upon
If a married man you dated.

Yes, he had his reasons
But I didn't hear him out
Now I'm the one who's left alone
Living with the doubt.

Lynne Taylor

SOMEDAY...

My love is silent as the mist
He lingers just beyond my view
Teasing lips that long to be kissed
Lonely heart draped in shades of blue

We pass through life in the same place
We share the same space in time
And yet I've never seen his face
No more than ever he's seen mine

Why must we walk this world apart?
Why don't our pathways ever meet?
I pray salvation for my heart
Someday, somehow, we'll be complete.

Tracy Palazzo

LONDON PRIDE

Once a proud city
That London of mine.
Beautiful buildings
The decor so fine.

Victorian splendour
So bright we could see,
The architects' skill
Over London still.

The times we remember
That Victorian splendour
With wide, busy streets,
A carriage and pair.

Monuments grand
Remind us of the times.
Victorian, Edwardian and then
Two world wars, men dying again.

Now in 2001
What have we done?
Dirt, grime and crime
Grow daily now in this London of mine.

Peoples of all nations now live
And visit here without a care
To what is happening over time
To this special city of mine.

Young people don't turn a hair
At the graffiti and rubbish everywhere.
Stop, you people, and look around
Where is my city that once was crowned?

Another century now begun
And in this year 2001
It is time to remember that city so fine
And return it to that London of mine.

Then we would see with no need to hide
That beautiful city that was once
London's pride.

Gwendoline Woodland

HAZEL AND ROSALIE

Two people I feel I trust,
I know about their friends, fear and lust.
Long summers spent on swings,
Hearing Roz and that song she sings.
They're my sisters and my friends,
A lasting love which never ends.
A special closeness only we share,
Winters spent without a care.
We're only young and our lives stretch before us,
Sitting together on the cold school bus.
We're friends and we've stuck together,
Been walking in every weather.
Hazel has a talent - a very special thing,
A 'feel' for everything - paw, claw and wing.
They're two people I know I can trust,
I have no choice - I know I must.

C Shepherd (14)

WOMAN OF WEALTH

I am a woman of great wealth and riches,
There is no fat, bulging bank account,
Nor, do I drip gold like decorations on a Christmas tree,
For my happiness is the wealth in me.

I have had my share of heartaches and pain,
But, I look to the positive and what I gain,
To have said, 'I love you,' and what I meant,
To those now gone and to Heaven went.

I take not for granted this Earthly life
Of the joy of being, a lover and wife,
I rise in the morning and look at the sun in the sky,
And I am glad I can see the trees and say 'Hi!'

I take pleasures from the small things, often hidden,
When I step off my horse of ambition, worry and strife,
I look around and see the true riches of life.

Friendships I have, are both near and far,
When I lie in bed at night, I see the star,
The guiding light of my inner self,
Now to me,
That is really wealth.

Carol Bradford

EVE

The disc
Horned,
with a corona,
of bronze tongues,
hissed impatience,
and soon became a crown.

The vein that broke out,
spotted as rust,
drew itself in line,
with the pregnant curve,
opening out,
the wound,
breathed,
into two.

Chimes spread their teeth,
bows of bells shook distantly,
and their mouths broke out,
into strange flowers,
and the hiss of long hair,
the whisper of short,
kissed.

The sky cleared,
threads coiled around her as vines,
the new dress billowed,
without breeze.

Her arms were crosses
and branches all the same
while light took away Adam's shape and form,
melting bones to dough.

The snake shrivelled to a question mark,
she blew away the ashes
stretched beyond sky,
her fingertips collected new yellow
while her face streamed with silver line,
and here she stood the new Eve,
diluting mesmerism,
reinventing the sun.

Debbie Graham

A HOUSEWIFE

I dust
I polish
I hoover
I wash
I iron
I mend
I sew
I cook
I wash pots
I scour pans
I scrub floors
I dig the garden
I sow the seeds
I hoe the weeds
I pick the fruit
I make the jam
I chop the wood
I carry the coal
I walk the dog
I feed the cat
I scatter the corn
I collect the eggs
I do this daily
Do you think
I am Superwoman?
No, I'm just
A housewife to you!

Olive Torkington

COSMIC ATTAINMENT

Reaching the top would be my goal
Feeling of freedom to set free my soul.
Rambling across the stepping stones of life
Ever too frequently towards the next epsilon of strife.
The feeling of fresh air upon my face
A new finding of self belief to embrace.
Nearly there, not many steps to go
Just like the sun my heart will glow.
Above the clouds I will be free
Favouring not laws but my own decree.
A part of me died, but is now reborn
With hand on heart I have sworn.
The passion is returning, full of fire
I am again learning to fulfil all desire.
The top is coming I'm nearly there
Anticipation taking away all my cares.
The climb has not been easy at all
I've held on tight so as not to fall.
To reach the top is so exhilarating
Looking on whilst adulating.
Squinting in the sunshine with idealism
I can forget the world and all its realism.
The top is in view, it is nearing
I can feel the freedom in the clearing.
On top of the world I will be
When that last step I can see.

Michaela W Moore

MARCH WOMAN

March is a woman
who can warm the snow,
and call the robins back.
But you'll have trouble
understanding her.
She won't tell you anything
except her ups and downs
in the wind.

Marion Schoeberlein

TIME BEHIND GLASS

Time ticks by in rapid fever,
Hands finger dying memory,
Second chance, seconds past,
Chime a silent cry for me.

Figures point as accusations,
Watch the hours regulate,
A piece of time behind glass features
Tells its secrets, same again.

Helen Marshall

MOTHER

Making a house into a home,
Mixing love and warmth and care!
Open all hours, and still is today:
Opportunities always there
To talk, discuss, laugh and joke;
Tell out our plans from the chair!
Hands clasping the cup of tea,
Hard working hands which want to share
Encouragement and enthusiasm;
Exit the doom! - let's prepare
Rewarding lives for all the family:
Rich in goals - to do and to dare!

Double the letters; double their worth -
As you read down and stare!
Doubling the strength of appreciation,
So, *Mother* deserves a spelling that's rare!

Denny Rhymer

PLEASURES OF SHE

Expose your way to human nature beyond
The weeping willow, hold her to your
Fevered breast, she, just she

Pluck a single feather from within your
Desire; lay it before you till cover of
Darkness does caress

Be fluent in the language of Love, indulge
Of the succulence in sameness, as one
Succumb to intrinsic pleasures, with she,
With she

Till wooded dawn shall sip, shall sip, beneath
Sleepy weeping willow did release, the sap
Of she, of she . . .

Papillion HVB

MY TREASURE

The starlight in your eyes
Is wonderful to see,
It starts a fizzy feeling
Deep inside of me

Every day I think of you
You always make me smile
Knowing you are in my life
Makes everything worthwhile

A very simple moment
Is worth its weight in gold
Now that you are with me
To touch, to have, to hold

A smile from you can make my day
It makes the dark clouds part
There's nothing that can conquer me
While you are in my heart

The times I have been lonely
Sad or down and blue
Disappear without trace
Each time I think of you

You challenge me
You stretch my mind
God sent this treasure
For me to find

You're always there
So kind and giving
Loving you
Makes life worth living!

Caroline Quinn

BLISSFULNESS

As I sit staring out of the window,
Watching a hundred lives walk by,
Not a care in the world,
And I can do nothing but sigh.

It's time like these that the world seems flawless,
The world is no longer daunting and scary,
I smile as I realise,
That the world can play fairly.

Everything happens for a reason,
I don't know why I'm here,
But I have a feeling I'm about of find out,
In this life I hold so dear.

Kimberly Harries

ON BEING A WOMAN

Two major ailments I suffer from -
a punctual womb and oestrogen.

Each bloody month it's always the same -
a slave to my hormones, devoted to pain.

Anguish and apathy besiege and conquer me -
a tragedy queen, I'm the perfect epitome.

Wouldn't you think after years of such malady
I've had reached a compromise between mind and body.

But I'm hopelessly imprisoned by Nature's laws.
How blessèd sounds the menopause!

Jane Baggaley

UNDERNEATH THE WOMAN

Just reminded today out of the blue
From one who doesn't have a clue.
It was a shock when I was
But what a jolt when I was no more
Not meant to be I resigned to the mind
Nature's way, imperfect perhaps.
Home I went to forge ahead
But then I was pulled back again
To that cold, white vacant place
Opened up just like that
Tied to a bed, no escape.
Life was dripped into me on the right
Drained out of me on the left
My heart was nowhere in-between
For my very soul was cut
Along with my lovely body.
Could not now blame Nature's creation
Only my own imperfect body.
Lying there wondering is this it
Or would life live within again?
A full woman glides by
With her carriage safely there
Why do they allow her to pass by
When I am in this empty state?
And why can I talk about my operation
But never my ectopic?

Eleanor McBride

EXCLUSIVE PICTURES

Reach for the TV remote
Robotic skeletons
Their fixed stare
Clothes hanging from them like drapes
Long, limp arms, exhausted from obsession
The 'toned midriff . . . '
The 'devout dieting . . . '
Inhuman.
Grotesque.
The systematic portrayal.
Now laugh, and then pretend you love having those thighs
Then ostentatiously smirk at their figures. Laugh. Wince. 'Disgusting!'
Yet turn your back from me
Frown sadly.
Then crane your head ritually over the table printed with coffee
                                                    mug rings
To delve into the glossy pages of yet another magazine.
Then let your mind wander aimlessly for the next hour and a half or so
Before finally discovering your fiery temperament and frantically trash
the kitchen cupboard
. . . Crumbling into an emotional heap
Of tears and insatiability.
Is this how you want to be?

Natalie Dybisz

CONTACT: PURE LINED AND BROKEN HEARTED
(For Melissa)

Still.
   - my soft weight brims with the thunder of hope -
She's looming over light and I'm surging on
    biscuit fields and beams
Propelling boundless energy.
Take this happy summer day and package it tight
                      Pure and invested
A dark corner to preserve your light
A brown paper package tied,
                   and back

Like our grip, hosting
'Raindrops on kittens' I thought
    And I was away
Flooding discourse into night
And the emerging condition of my aching fist in *chest*
Drag me over and all around
                   The back streets of this
Familiar and revolving town.
This is yours and mine,   *this time*
And the moments we live in
             we grow.

First up -
The lightning fix of hope
And sockets of heartfelt clarity
           Whispers and breathing
Always soothed this battered soul
Leave me just enough room for my shoulders
           to support backbones
               to sprout wings
     And smother the rest of me whole.

Rachel Rakewell

FEMALE SINGLEDOM

Sometimes I feel I'm living life like Bridget Jones' Diary,
Never quite in control of what's going on, well at least not entirely.
I over eat and self indulge, whilst worrying about my weight,
Constantly living, so it seems in a hazy drunken state.
I keep searching for a Mr Right but choosing Mr Wrong,
Whose idea of the perfect date consists of beer, footie and a thong!
But my quest for romance isn't over, my life story isn't yet through.
As I hold a bar of choccie in one hand and I've a scratch card I have
still to do.

Cassandra Smith

BAGGAGE

*(This poem was inspired by 'I Wish We'd All Been Ready' -
Larry Norman, Christian musician and singer)*

Will I see a flickering candle to guide me to the Light
If only I knew which way was home
I run to catch a ghost-train but there is no sign of life
The gospel train I missed to take me home.

Will I find the road to Freedom as I walk the seething street
If only I knew which way was home
I hug a heavy handbag weighed down with purse and pills
The gospel train I missed and so I roam.

A rolling stone gathers all the garbage down the hill
If only I new which way was home
The clutter closes in and the shutter shouts 'Hooray!'
I missed the gospel train to take me home.

Distractions of the present plus nostalgia of the past
If only I knew which way was home
There is no sign of *life* on this mad highway to Hell
The gospel train pulled out the night before.

Where is the burning bush that brought the truth from God
If only I knew which way was home
Deserted by the crowds but the spaces form a queue
The train has left on time and I'm alone.

Freedom's finger beckons yet still I stand alone
If only I knew which way was home
I weep and wail in misery whilst laughing luggage leers
Weighed down I drown my sorrows in the rain.

Where is that gospel train . . .?

Judy Studd

FIRST TIME MOTHER

Anticipating, waiting, straining to show the prize,
The mother.
Through the door,
Face betrays the hidden well.
Hesitating hands part with the precious one.

Soft flame kindles nature's movements,
Melting face and arms and voice.
Sleeping bud unfurled to gaping splendour.
Whispered awe.

Stella M

TICK-TOCK

Most of the time life is so repetitive,
The same old thing every day,
And so, the weeks roll on and on,
Into a never-ending sea of routine.

A lot of folk I'm sure,
Would like to get off this carousel,
And do exactly as they would like to do,
Including myself.

I would love to flee the life I know,
And drown in a timeless wonder.
Freedom from time which dictates my
                                    whole being,
Time which demands me to get up, eat,
                                    work, sleep.

The above are purely wasteful thoughts,
Or are they? I ask myself.
If I had the courage I would try and answer.
To experience something else before time
                                    itself runs out
And my life becomes, but just a dream.

Anita Bodle

HOUSEWIFE'S LAMENT

She's a housewife and a mother but no intellect can claim,
Though she has so many talents for her title rings with shame.
She's a cook for all and sundry, (does the children's homework too)
With the washing and the ironing while she makes a dress or two!

She must fetch and carry children with their friends to school and clubs,
Is a chauffeur for her husband when he's drinking in the pubs.
She's a hostess to his colleagues whom she entertains with skill,
She's a cleaner, teacher, tailor and a nurse when they are ill.

Introductions are insulting, she's known as her husband's wife
Or the mother of her children - no one thinks she has a life
When she might grab precious moments on her own she can write,
When profundity of thinking and intelligence unite.

Children grow more independent in the normal course of time,
So she'll find herself employment, but what really is a crime
Is that chores are always waiting till the day that she expires
While a man always looks forward to the day that he retires.

When he'll potter in the garden and he'll potter in the shed
And will watch the television every morning from his bed
But a woman - up and working (for the chores she can't suspend),
Should be titled 'Wonder-Woman' for she works right to the end!

Joy Saunders

A Woman's Point Of View

Who is my true love,
Who is it to be,
Where on earth will he be
        waiting for me.
To whom does he belong,
Will he fill my heart with song.
Is he short, tall, dark or fair,
Will he be kindly will, will he care.
Will he try to please me,
Only time will tell.
I will have to be patient, and wait
For time to pass by, to see
If I get the perfect match for me.
Come true love, let us meet
A perfect marriage would be great.
Whom does he belong to, who is he to be,
I will be patient and wait and see.

Jean Nicholls

RECOGNITION
(Thanks to the dedicated staff at Peterborough Hospital)

Women of the universe
in every walk of life
every child's mother
to every man a wife

To stand up and be counted
we guard a hidden fear
this cannot be important
I've lived another year

Great women of this century
have fought this to the end
in their fight to deal with it
they learn it's claimed a friend

We need to make a statement
there's no family history
my mother's alive and kicking
why should it come to me?

We watch the campaigns rolling
the warning's very clear
it lurks around the corner
and increases every year

We must not take it lightly
thank God it isn't me
the reality of this message
Is . . . Tomorrow it could be

Wipe away the stigma
embarrassment has no place
it does not pick and choose
the age, the creed the race

So, ladies please be counted
let's make a lot of fuss
we want the world to know
Breast Cancer's killing us!

Alexandria Phipps (Diagnosed February 2001)

A DEEP WINTER'S LOVE

Deep winter's love, last longest.
You met, then hugged
to keep each other warm.
Snuggled together, passionately kissing
as snowflake's dance
in the wind around you.
Wispy, they glide down
and alight on your clothes,
cold cheeks and both of your noses.
Melt, they do, fast
on inflamed lips
heated from hearts of passion.
Sparkling, are the hard glassy
diamonds of crisp snowflakes
frozen on top of night's snow.
As pure and as virtuous
as the diamond ring,
he knows he will place on her hand.
A deep winter's love
raging and heart warming, on fire,
even when the icy wind's
glaze, four moonstruck eyes.

Susan Carole Roberts

The Woman's War

There was me once, whether you believe it or not,
There was me once but I think you forgot,
The lock cannot turn without the key,
And I know now that you need me!
My life is mine and mine to live,
I threw away those shackles as I threw away your sieve,
And your cleaner and your kitchen gloves,
I hope you realise how far I have gone now my love,

And that was a word you would never use,
And I played your game and now you lose,
My darling, you are not that any more,
My dear you made me fight your war,
I thought my revolution was in the past,
But those chauvinist attitudes tend to last,
Your gothic ways made me change,
Now I'm whole again and taking you over in the fast lane,
I won this battle and I won the war,
I thank you for being you,
Now I am so much more.

Cathryn Harman

THE CREATION OF WOMAN

The creation of Eve was to be truly unique.
No other creation could match this might feat.
She was to be a companion to Adam.
A compliment to him.
Not a lesser creature
Or a second-class citizen
But a person whose intelligence matched his.
Someone to share his deepest thoughts.
A person to turn to in times of distress.
They were to work as a team.
No need to compete one against the other.
For she had a special role.
A role to be considered with respect by all.
She had the ability to bring forth life.
To be tender and show deep compassion.
To fill the world with her laughter.
To express her sadness with tears.
Working hard in her family.
In the community.
With no special bonuses or overtime pay.
Although not as physically strong as her husband.
She had a superior inner strength to endure.
This one was to be called *'Woman'*.

Sonja M Bonitto

SOUTH STACK

A past has returned to haunt my tomorrows,
I must step back, to a time of childhood days, once more,
to see the steep drop of your craggy cliffs,
embellished by fleawort and thrift,
where oystercatchers stop by,
where guillemots and tern swoop down to poise upon your
warning beacon, bethroned in the Irish Sea.

Too soon nimbus clouds gather.
I watch, as a foolhardy fishing boat,
with lantern swinging at the prow, awaits
to haul its catch;
then, sensing danger from a freshening breeze,
seeks refuge from dark passages of gloomy
awesome caves.

A red sun, descends into the horizon of a lucent sea,
waiting to rise, in yet another day;
when artists, twitchers and the like,
will come to sketch and snapshots take,
of your august majesty.

South Stack, you haunt my every day with bygone memories.
Long since gone the old familiar faces,
that graced your shores in halcyon days.
Replaced by geological day trippers
chipping, at your soul.

I shall come to you one day at twilight,
when darkened hours are few,
and linger, in approving silence of the day's end.
Only then, as I breathe the salty air of Holy Island,
will my nostalgia by satisfied.

Margaret Frow

FLORENCE DAISY

Born in 1905 when life was very hard,
The eldest of four children living, home in a courtyard.
To see a baby sister die, at a very tender age
Not to dwell here too long better turn the page.

She and her younger sister worked, both upstairs and down.
In service to the Bomza family in old London town.
She was very bright and at just fifteen years of age,
Was cashier in a tea shop to help the family wage.

Later as a 'Nippy' served refreshments daily,
In Lyons Corner House outside The Old Bailey.
In the thirties Lyons opened for Coventrians to be fed,
Both sisters worked there, met young men and wed.

During the November Blitz, my dad was a warden,
In the local ARP, was part of the area cordon.
After this night of horror a decision they both made,
'We'd better have a family' and so their plans they laid.

For if he was taken from her, she could not be sad
With a little living reminder of the happiness they'd had.
Both saw the war out I am glad to say,
And I too, as their child still to this day.

He had a massive heart attack at the age of forty-two,
Her family and friends rallied round her, but they always knew
Her religious belief would help her ride, whatever stormy weather
Our very many times, of shared, hard knocks together

Then, for a few short years she married and cared for
An elderly family friend, and when he died, alone she saw time,
                                      pass by her door.
She has now passed on aged ninety, near my fifty-fourth birthday,

She was my mum, my friend, and I loved her and I miss her.

Sheila Bates

PRINCESS

Sleep now princess of Celtic praise
And rest within your isle of childhood dreams.
You were upon this earth too short a time
  and no one ever thought that you would leave it seems.
Now each night another star shines
It is brighter than the other stars
It has only just arrived!

The Welsh have lost a jewel in their Celtic crown
And the day that you departed so many minds were blown.
Your smile and your compassion will live forever more
And when your name is mentioned there shall be an ever-open door.

The world has mourned your passing
From the east unto the west,
And there will be no doubt fair lass as you walk those
      pastures green you will be an honoured guest.
So sit amongst the angles and take your final rest.

Derek J Morgan

ZOE

Dear Zoe stole my breath away
With charm and love and grace.
I long to stroke her every day
And see her pretty face.

She trusted me in every way,
She'd run to greet me with such glee.
Oh! I could never say her nay
Her joy was there for all to see.

Her faithful friendship filled each day
But God my darling did not live.
Her presence round me's here to stay
And all the love that she did give.

I miss her funny little ways
The balls she kicked are still around
I see them through a tearful haze.
They are all about me on the ground.

She'd look at me with soulful eyes.
No sign of suffering did she show.
I daily look and search the skies.
I know she's there - but where?

Betty Smyth

WILL WE NOT MEET AGAIN?
(We are both almost forty-one)

Desire did feel like flowers on rain
There was nearly youthful fun,
One quarter century later
Her husband's children would be grown,
Gone the ambition to make her
A loving wife; my own.

But now my dreams are dim
(Illusions I have none?)
The young man I was within
Lies a broken one.
Maybe she re-lives the day
A past the years have faded
But in the heart the memory's stayed
Through plans and dreams belated.

Simon Morton

THE GYPSY YOUTH ACROSS THE WAY

To disturb our quiet respectability and tidiness
Houses with pride in gardens well tended -
Many occupied by elderly people who had brought up their families
in the self-same house.
Came, a wild young man, living like a gypsy.
Windows wide open, curtains of uncertain white, blowing - billowing
in the road, a wilderness garden.
Motorbikes, 'his and friends'' - revving. Congregating. A lot of
grumbles from neighbours - but backbiting I cannot abide - bring
things into the open!
I thought it over carefully - perhaps a letter through the letterbox
requesting him to call.
Answered by his presence the same evening.
His hair shoulder length, the modern attire of jeans and sweatshirt.
I watched him come, wondering the outcome.
I asked him his name, would he come in for a chat
Talking of previous inhabitants, and that now a window - my outlook
did matter greatly.
He listened politely, and when requested stood up to look at his home,
the garden piled high with logs, delivered after the storm
A tarpaulin covered them - very ugly.
Silence - no hassle - but his remark
'I have to look at your modern flats, which I think are very ugly - I am
a country man - I like cottages -'
Actually - mine is one of a block of four flats - well built and designed
by an architect - in fact I am quite pleased with the appearance.
The lawn in front - a driveway - and flowerbeds beneath the
front windows.
There is also a garden and lawn at the rear and four garages and a
fair-sized yard.
I countered with - 'The architecture is good, if you prefer country
cottages - why do you not leave and work in the country.
As a widow - yours and other houses opposite are my landscape
and mean a lot to me.'
A gentle countryside to his nature took over.
'I will clear up my garden slowly - I promise.'

The next day - I took him one of my 'landscapes' - he had told me
he sketched.
He was overjoyed and said he would frame it - I said, 'One good turn
deserves another . . .'
The green tarpaulin was removed and gradually - very - the tidiness has
taken over - including a new wooden seat under the bay window
No one ever sits on it - but obviously it is a gesture!
This all goes to show - straight forward approach is the best way -
And there is a good side in everyone.

Madeline Chase Thomas

PLATFORM 9 - THE MOURNING AFTER

After Everest and K2
life was an anticlimax.
'This is the price you pay,' I mused
as the train arrived at the station.
'Climber bored' came the cry.
I was. And I did.

Vincent Hefter

SOMEWHERE

Somewhere in the silence of a vale
Daydreams a delightful daffodil.
                    But not here.

Somewhere shaded, water lily floats
And emerald flames from a thousand sylvan throats.
                            But not here.

Somewhere from still waters hills rise high,
Bear crimson clouds which gleam in a dusky sky.
                        But not here.

Elizabeth Stephens

PRIDE OF PLACE

'Education's a fine thing,' said Mother,
'Just take a look at your older brother.
He has learned to read and learned to write,
You have to admit that he's very bright.
His thirst for knowledge was forever burning
So he's been away to the halls of learning.
He'd got all his O levels in this and in that
By passing each exam that he'd ever sat.
He has strived through the night and all
Through each day,
Determined that education would finally pay.
Now in society he has such a fine role,
He's got pride of place,
In the queue,
For his dole.'

G Craven

THE TEMP

Do your work - hurry on with it,
or you'll be in front of moody old Pitt.
See your work's done. Do it right,
old Pitt's eyes have got you in sight.

Hurry. Make sure your task is done,
you're here to work - not for fun.
Too much work and lots to do,
no time for absence, no time for flu.

Work much faster, work much harder,
you're earning money to fill your larder.
Old Pitt's watching from the door,
looking forlorn, looking sore.

You're working well, doing much better,
but I must sadly give you this letter.
You've done the work you came here for,
but I must now show you the door.

Your work's now over - thanks a bunch!
We'll say goodbye after lunch.
Worry not my son, but leave in cheer,
we'll see you again this time next year.

Steve Kettlewell

MEMORIES

To take a photograph is to capture a moment in all its glory.
To hold a photograph is to cherish the past like it were a story.
To see a photograph is to be drawn into a world of splendour.
But the finest moment is being in the photograph with a moment
                                                        to endure.
So fine is that moment, that you will look back in years to come
And realise you have made a memory to last forever.

Tracey Burgon

RANGER 2, 3

I am the deep space astronaut
The hero for all I was worth
After light years deep out in the universe
It's time to make my return to earth.

Ground control they do not hear my calls
Maybe it's a storm or deep static
On my final approach there's a lump in my throat
My trajectory is set, I'm switching to automatic.

It appears that I've been gone for too long
With a deep breath I open the door
Something is different, something has changed
Somehow it doesn't feel like home anymore.

The sun is so big it fills the sky
Earth is scorched and the air so hot
Has man contrived a plan to survive?
From all I can see, most probably not.

'This is Ranger 2, 3, do you hear me? Copy.'
My hails they rise to a shout
On the scorched planet face, I'm the alien race
'This is Ranger 2, 3 signing off, over, out.'

David Whitehouse

REACH OUT

Reach out your hand and come to me,
No matter where you are.
I'll guide you through each stormy night,
Until you reach your star.

Don't think about the rocky road
That lies ahead of you.
Reach out to me and you will find
A friend so loyal and true.

I can see you've travelled far
From the lines within your face.
You need a place where you belong,
To be loved and needed in a place.

So rest your head my weary friend
And rest until the dawn.
We'll walk away from loneliness,
To a place we've never known.

Where you will find a perfect peace
With someone that you love.
And I will say 'Goodbye' to you
So go with love from the good Lord above.

Ian Proctor

AN EXILE'S DREAM

Each night I walk the road that leads to Ireland,
Bridges bridged by bridges in my dreams,
And I stroll the Shannon waters that are my land,
And stop to rest by tranquil flowing streams.
The songs that touch so deep and pull my heart strings,
I sing so proud though I an exile be.
I've danced with colleens fair at last light gleaming,
And drove the road and miles down to Tralee,
To hear accordions play by flickering firelight,
Shall my soul pass through old Ireland just once more
And drink the lovely black stuff, Ireland's nectar?
Awake the dream and sail me to thy shore.
There are many exiles living o're the waters,
With bonds that call them back to that dear land.
And I've sat beside the loch at Limavady,
Watched Belfast raise the morning at first hand,
Kissed an Irish rose, for Ireland's full of roses,
Walked amongst the forty shades of green,
Lay in heather on the hills of Kerry,
Sailed my boat on Galway so serene,
And where the shamrock grows so shall my heart be,
For I left you there upon her lovely shore,
And bridges bridged by bridges they will lead me,
To walk upon her holy ground once more.

J Brohee

MEMORY

They sent you Oh so far away
On the day that would have been our wedding day
A job to do, a war to be won
Before our married life had begun.

You were a big Scotsman, wore your kilt with pride
I watched you march away, Oh the tears I cried.
Your letters came, they said you were well
And doing your bit amongst the hell.

I missed you so, I wrote each day
As he promised as he went away.
One day no letter came, I began to worry
My mum told me 'Dear don't be in a hurry.'

'Am I never to see you again?' I cried
And I was right, my big Jock had died.
Now all I have are moments to remember
My wedding dress and a date in November.

Marjorie Wagg

SUMMER

Blue skies, lapping waves
Carefree summer days.
Kites flying in the air
Strawberries and cream, Oh so good.
Roses' perfume wafts in the breeze
All these things we wish for.
For holidays, home or abroad
Buckets and spades,
Splashing in the sea,
Getting a tan
Girls in summer wear
Boys stare
Summer's here!

Gillian Robson